Leave the World Behind
The Poetry of the Temple

THOMAS L. KAY

© 2018 Thomas L. Kay

All rights reserved. This book or any portion thereof may not be reproduced or used in any manner whatsoever without the express written permission of the publisher except for the use of brief quotations in a book review or scholarly journal.

Cover Image by Kathryn F. Kay

Contents

3	Leave The World Behind
4	The Temple
4	Psalms 24:3-6
5	A Simple Question
5	Temple Marriage
6	To Serve Within
6	The Temple Shines
7	Psalms 27:4-8
7	Find Yourself
8	Simple, Beautiful, and Sacred
8	The Veil Between
9	Eternal Marriage
9	The Beauty and the Glory
9	The Temple Brings Perspective
10	Grateful to Serve
10	Temple Service

11	May I Remember
11	Serving in the Temple
11	Doctrine & Covenants 109:80
12	Psalms 134:1-2
12	Temple Tuesday
13	In the Temple
13	A Pleasure to Serve
13	Every Temple Night
14	Remember
14	Veil Worker
15	Locker Assignment
15	Let the Temple Pass Through Us
15	Isaiah 22:23
16	Temple Time
16	Exodus 40:12-13
17	Marriage in the Temple
17	A Reminder
18	The Temple in the Storm

18	Nearness to the Temple
18	In the Temple More
19	A Place of Peace
19	Thy Servants
20	Don't Make Me Leave
20	The Symbol of Our Membership
20	Isaiah 61:10
21	Temple Insights
21	A Vision and a Focus
22	A Gift from God
22	In a New Light
23	Between Earth and Heaven
23	Help Me Remember
23	Acts 5:42
24	Dressed in White
24	No Other Church
25	In His House

25	Within These Temple Walls
26	1 John 2:27
26	Not Surprised
27	Temple Proof
27	A Piece of Heaven
27	Psalms 122:1, 9
28	To Serve Thee
28	I Saw Jesus
29	The Veil
29	I Heard the Truth
30	Psalms 42:4
30	To Be Here
30	Go Onward
31	A Heavenly Space
31	Eternity in Mirrors
31	A Sacred, Quiet Place
32	It Proves It
32	Do Not Neglect

33	We Do This Work
33	Close to Me
33	Leviticus 8:6-7
34	I Thank Thee
34	The Most Sacred Place
35	Alone in the Temple
35	Psalms 95:1-3
36	I Came into the Temple
36	What the Temple Is
37	The Place Between
37	Hebrews 10:19-20
38	Order, Ordain, Ordinance
38	Close to Him
39	Doctrine & Covenants 109:8
39	We Kneel Before The Altar
40	It's All Relative
40	Psalms 23:6

40 Heaven

41 Isaiah 2:2-3

Introduction

A temple is literally a house of the Lord, a holy sanctuary in which sacred ceremonies and ordinances of the gospel are performed by and for the living and also in behalf of the dead. A place where the Lord may come, it is the most holy of any place of worship on the earth. Only the home can compare with the temple in sacredness.

Whenever the Lord has had a people on the earth who will obey His word, they have been commanded to build temples in which the ordinances of the gospel and other spiritual manifestations that pertain to exaltation and eternal life may be administered. (LDS Bible Dictionary). Additional references include *The House of the Lord* by James E. Talmage, *The Holy Temple* by Boyd K. Packer, and *Through Temple Doors* by John K. Edmunds.

These poems were written from my experience in the temples of The Church of Jesus Christ of Latter-day Saints. For more than 45 years I have attended and worshiped in the temple. For the last three years I have also served in the Bountiful Utah Temple. These poems reflect my love, insight, and joy in serving in The House of the Lord.

The temple is the link between the seeming chaos and dissolution of this temporal world and the beautiful configuration (cosmos) and permanence of the eternal order. The mystique of the temple lies in its extension to other worlds; it is the reflection on earth of the heavenly order, and the power that fills it comes from above.

Hugh Nibley

Ancient writers assure us repeatedly that the temple is the earthly type of Zion, a holy place removed from contact with the outer world, set apart for ordinances from which the world is excluded.

Hugh Nibley

Leave the World Behind

I will leave
the tumult
of the world

I will leave
the world behind

I will go
to where
the Spirit is

in God's temple
I will find

I will find
the things
the world can't give

I'll escape
this mortal strife

I will find
the things
that matter most

I will hear
the words
of life.

February 26, 2006

The Temple

The temple is an anchor
in an ever shifting world
When tempests rage around us
gospel standards are unfurled

The temple is a beacon
in a starless, darkened night
When fog and dread surround us
there still shines a steadfast light

The temple is a harbor
from a never ending storm
A refuge and a covert
where the Son shall keep us warm.

October 6, 1996

Psalms 24:3-6

Who shall ascend into the hill
of the Lord? or who shall stand
in his holy place?

He that hath clean hands and
a pure heart; who hath not lifted up
his soul unto vanity, nor sworn deceitfully.

He shall receive the blessing from the Lord,
and righteousness from the God of his salvation.

This is the generation of them that seek him,
that seek thy face.

May 31, 2018

A Simple Question

The question
is quite simple
This isn't
a hard case

With reference
to the temple
which way does
your tent face?

May 24, 2005

Temple Marriage

A temple marriage
in the House of the Lord
is beautifully simple
and simply profound

It binds the new husband
and wife together
It binds the new couple
to God

By keeping all
of their covenants
they grow closer
to each other
and to Him.

March 21, 2010

To Serve Within

To serve within
God's temple
like those
of ancient days

To feel
the Holy Spirit
to worship
and to pray.

June 21, 2016

The Temple Shines

The Holy Temple
The House of the Lord
stands dedicated
to the Lord

Celestial rooms
all filled with light
Majestic shine
in darkest night.

February 13, 1995

Psalms 27:4-8

One thing have I desired of the Lord,
that will I seek after; that I may dwell
in the house of the Lord all the days
of my life, to behold the beauty of the Lord,
to enquire in his temple.

For in the time of trouble he shall hide me
in his pavilion: in the secret of his tabernacle
shall he hide me; he shall set me up upon a rock.

And now shall mine head be lifted up
above mine enemies round about me:
therefore will I offer in his tabernacle
sacrifices of joy; I will sing, yea, I will sing
praises unto the Lord.

Hear, O Lord, when I cry with my voice:
have mercy upon me, and answer me.

When thou saidst, Seek ye my face;
my heart said unto thee, Thy face,
Lord, will I seek.

May 29, 2018

Find Yourself

It is when
you find yourself
in the temple

that you will find
so much more
of yourself.

October 14, 2007

Simple, Beautiful, and Sacred

Simple
Beautiful
Sacred

The Temple
of the Lord

Committed
Faithful
Righteous

The keepers
of His word.

May 30, 2017

The Veil Between

The veil between
this earth and heaven
grows thin when this work
is done

We often sense
the dead are near
as we serve them
and the Son.

August 15, 2017

Eternal Marriage

For time and all eternity
forever and today
to seal our love
all dressed in white
and wed in God's own way.

November 5, 1999

The Beauty and Glory

The beauty of the temple
is the covenants we have made
The glory of the gospel
is the lives that Jesus saves.

February 6, 2000

The Temple Brings Perspective

The temple brings perspective
within a world of strife
It focuses our minds and hearts
what matters most in life.

February 29, 2000

Grateful to Serve

How grateful I am
to be able to serve
in the House of the Lord

Each week I leave
this world and spend
the evening in peace

I grow closer
to my Savior
and my Heavenly Father

I feel closer
to the Spirit as I serve
within these walls.

June 3, 2015

Temple Service

To serve the Lord
each Tuesday
to be within
these walls

To feel
the Holy Spirit
To magnify
my call.

September 15, 2015

May I Remember

May I always remember
who I represent
in thy temple this day

To act as He would
if He were here
To follow in His way.

April 12, 2016

Serving in the Temple

I love to serve
in the temple
To serve with
good people that care

I love to ponder what
I have seen and heard
and what I've felt
in answers to prayers.

May 10, 2016

Doctrine & Covenants 109:80

And let these, thine anointed ones,
be clothed with salvation, and
thy saints shout aloud for joy.
Amen, and Amen.

June 5, 2018

Psalms 134:1-2

Behold, bless ye the Lord,
all ye servants of the Lord,
which by night stand
in the house of the Lord.

Lift up your hands
in the sanctuary,
and bless the Lord.

May 2, 2017

Temple Tuesday

Tuesday night
is always a good one
I look forward
to it each week

It is the time
that I serve
in the House of the Lord
and a blessing
I want to keep.

May 17, 2016

In the Temple

When I serve
in the temple
I feel and see all
in white

I am a part
of all the past
and those within
the light.

May 17, 2016

A Pleasure to Serve

It is great to serve
in the temple
A warm glow grows
inside of my soul

Tuesday night
is the best of my week now
Life is full and this work
makes me whole.

September 27, 2016

Every Temple Night

Each night that I am
in the temple
impressions come to me
Illumination from the Spirit
intersects eternity.

November 22, 2016

Remember

Slowly
Softly
Reverently
Prayerfully
Distinctly

This is how
a veil worker
should speak.

May 2, 2017

Veil Worker

Be ye clean
inside and out

Remember who
you represent

Smile inside
and outside, too

Be perfect in what
you say and do.

April 10, 2015

Locker Assignment

Let's just say
that they call it
"locker assignment"
so that is what I do

but I also get
to tell people
where to go
and I admit
that's enjoyable, too.

May 9, 2017

Let the Temple Pass Through Us

Let the temple
pass through us
as we pass
through temple doors

Let the Spirit
teach our hearts
and bring us back
for more.

January 23, 2005

Isaiah 22:23

And I will fasten him as
a nail in the sure place; and
he shall be for a glorious
throne to his father's house.

June 5, 2018

Temple Time

It's temple time
a time for prayer
a time for showing
God you care

A time to learn
a time for growth
a time to worship
the Lord of Hosts.

February 6, 2005

Exodus 40:12-13

And thou shalt bring Aaron
and his sons unto the door
of the tabernacle of the congregation,
and wash them with water.

And thou shalt put upon Aaron
the holy garments, and anoint him,
and sanctify him.

May 29, 2018

Marriage in the Temple

For time
and all eternity
Forever
and today

We kneel
across the altar
and marry
in God's way.

March 14, 2006

A Reminder

The temple
helps reminds us
of the things
that matter most

To worship
God the Father
and Jesus Christ
the Lord of Hosts.

March 15, 2005

The Temple in the Storm

I often think
the temple shines
the brightest
in a storm

And when
I come inside of it
the Spirit
keeps me warm.

March 31, 2006

Nearness to the Temple

The temple is
so near to me

How close am I
to it?

May 7, 2006

In the Temple More

The more you are
in the temple
the deeper
you will grow

and closer
to the Savior
What power
you will know.

January 14, 2007

A Place of Peace

It is a place
of peace and joy
where thy sweet spirit
dwells

A holy place
a holy time
where hearts and spirits
swell.

September 17, 2007

Thy Servants

May all thy servants
go forth
from this house
armed with thy power
that thy name
be upon them
and thy glory
be unfurled

May all thy servants
go forth
from this house
to bear the truth
that all those
who listen
will assert
this is thy work.

June 25, 2007

Don't Make Me Leave

I do not want
to leave it
the temple
of the Lord

I only want
to stay here
and ponder more
His words.

February 18, 2008

The Symbol of Our Membership

The temple is
the symbol
of our membership

It stands for what
we would like
to become.

February 10, 2008

Isaiah 61:10

For he hath clothed me with the
garments of salvation, he hath
covered me with the robe of
righteousness.

February 17, 2018

Temple Insights

To wash
anoint
and sanctify

To covenant
to be true

To live your life
in faithfulness

To endure well
until life's through.

July 13, 2008

A Vision and a Focus

The temple
gives us a vision
of who we really are

The temple focuses
our attention
on what we can become.

August 17, 2008

A Gift from God

The temple is
a gift from God
Do not deny God's gift

He wants us
to come unto Him
He knows what is
best for us

He knew us before
we came to earth
He knows our joys
and pains

His House is where
He will help us know
His truths He will explain.

May 11, 2009

In a New Light

And now I see
the temple
in a new
and wonderful light

And now I do
appreciate
the atonement
of Jesus Christ.

July 5, 2009

Between Earth and Heaven

The temple is
the House of the Lord
It is the place
between earth and heaven

The Spirit thunders
this to me
How much hope
my Lord has given.

September 15, 2015

Help Me Remember

Please bless me
to remember
as I serve
in the House of the Lord

that I represent
the Savior
and to be pure
in mind and heart.

April 5, 2016

Acts 5:42

And daily in the temple,
and in every house,
they ceased not to teach
and preach Jesus Christ.

February 28, 2017

Dressed in White

When all are
dressed in white
and all stand
ready to serve

The Lord's work
will go forth
as covenants
are fulfilled.

May 3, 2016

No Other Church

No other Church
has done this work
to seek out and
redeem the dead

But our church does
with authority from Christ
and we know by whom
we are led.

May 10, 2016

In His House

To think that I
am in His House
the Temple of
the Lord

To feel the spirit
of this work
and search
His holy word.

May 10, 2016

Within These Temple Walls

The time goes quickly
as I serve within
these temple walls

The beauty of those
dressed in white
who walk these
sacred halls.

May 10, 2016

1 John 2:27

But the anointing which ye
have received of him abideth
in you, and ye need not that
any man teach you: but as the
same anointing teacheth you
of all things, and is truth,
and is no lie, and even as it
hath taught you, ye shall
abide in him.

January 17, 2018

Not Surprised

I would not be surprised
if I saw Him in a hall
or I saw Him in a room
I was in

I would not be surprised
but would be grateful
and with tears of love
I would kneel and bow to Him.

May 17, 2016

Temple Proof

The temple proves
this Church is true
It proves this Church
is true

The sealing power
that seals us His
and links us
as we do.

June 14, 2016

A Piece of Heaven

The temple is
a piece of heaven
a piece of heaven
on earth

It is where
I can go and learn
the things that are
of most worth.

August 13, 2016

Psalms 122:1, 9

I was glad when they said unto me,
Let us go into the house of the Lord.

Because of the house of the Lord
our God I will seek thy good.

May 29, 2018

To Serve Thee

To work inside
the temple
To serve both
night and day

To represent
the Father
and the life,
the truth, the way.

August 23, 2016

I Saw Jesus

I saw Jesus
in the temple
in a painting
blessing a child

Then I saw Him
teaching women
expounding scriptures
to their minds

I saw Jesus
in the temple
in a painting
healing the lame

Then I saw Him
in clouds of glory
descending to earth
for the second time.

August 30, 2016

The Veil

To approach
the Father
we must go
through the veil

and the veil
we go through
is Jesus Christ

The only way
we can return
to God
is through our Savior.

August 30, 2016

I Heard The Truth

I heard the truth
taught in the temple
I heard the truth
and smiled within

I knew that God
knew who I was
and knew what
I now know.

September 6, 2016

Psalms 42:4

When I remember these things,
I pour out my soul in me: for I
had gone with the multitude, I went
with them to the house of God,
with the voice of joy and praise,
with a multitude that kept holy-day.

May 30, 2018

To Be Here

To be here
in thy holy house
to be here
to serve Thee

To feel thy Spirit
within these walls
and seek eternity.

September 13, 2016

Go Onward

It is not clear
when the Savior
will come
But each Tuesday
his Spirit is near

I look forward
to his Second Coming
I go onward
and serve without fear.

September 27, 2016

A Heavenly Space

The temple is
a heavenly space
where we can draw
nearer to Thy face.

November 22, 2016

Eternity in Mirrors

Eternity in mirrors
extending without end
forever reaching forward
in steps we must ascend.

December 14, 2016

A Sacred, Quiet Place

The temple is
the House of the Lord
a sacred, quiet place

Where we make covenants
with our God
and seek His holy face,

March 21, 2017

It Proves It

I testify
that family history
proves that this work
is true

and when we find
those that we love
the temple comes
into view.

July 11, 2017

Do Not Neglect

A place to look
most forward to
A time when we
reflect

The temple is
the House of God
This place do not
neglect.

August 15, 2017

We Do This Work

We do this work
for those now dead
for those whose names
we have found

And as we do
this work for them
the Spirit will
abound.

August 15, 2017

Close to Me

There have been times
when I do this work
that the dead seem
close to me

And I sense that
they accept my work
and that we will embrace
eternity.

August 15, 2017

Leviticus 8:6-7

And Moses brought Aaron
and his sons, and washed them
with water.
And he put upon him the coat,
and girded him with the girdle,
and clothed him with the robe.

January 17, 2018

I Thank Thee

Heavenly Father
Thou great Elohim
How thankful am I
for this time and this place
where I can serve Thee

To work within
these holy walls
the lighted halls
and rooms
To serve behind
the sacred veil
where faithful saints
return.

August 15, 2017

The Most Sacred Place

The most sacred place
in the temple
is where I am called
to serve

To represent the Father
and test those who
come to obtain
what they deserve.

August 15, 2017

Alone in the Temple

I found myself alone
in the temple
walking down a hall
when this thought came
to me

"I am in the House
of the Lord" and then,
"I would not be surprised
if I saw Him around the next corner"

Although this did not happen,
the Spirit whispered to me,
"This is His house and
He comes here."

October 1, 2017

Psalms 95:1-3

O come, let us sing unto the Lord:
let make a joyful noise to the rock
of our salvation.

Let us come before his presence
with thanksgiving, and make a
joyful noise unto him with psalms.

For the Lord is a great God, and
a great King above all gods.

May 29, 2018

I Came into the Temple

I came into
the temple

I came to seek
the Lord

I sought to feel
the Spirit

I left to search
His word.

December 26, 2017

What the Temple Is

The temple is
the House of the Lord
the place between
earth and heaven

The more we attend
the closer we feel
How bright is
the Spirit that's given.

January 2, 2018

The Place Between

The place between
earth and heaven
is the place that
I want to be

To covenant
with our Father
for all eternity.

January 9, 2018

Hebrews 10:19-20

Having therefore, brethren,
boldness to enter into
the holiest by the blood
of Jesus,

By a new and living way,
which he hath consecrated
for us, through the veil,
that is to say, his flesh.

August 23, 2016

Order, Ordain, Ordinance

Order

Ordain

Ordinance

Order–To put in ranks or rows, in proper sequence or relationship.

Ordain–The process of putting things in rows of proper relationship.

Ordinance–The ceremony by which things are put in order.

January 17, 2018
(from Boyd K. Packer, The Holy Temple, p. 165)

Close to Him

The temple
brings us close to Him
if we will go
in faith

If we will do
what He has asked
we will receive
His strength.

February 25, 2018

Doctrine & Covenants 109:8

Organize yourselves; prepare
every needful thing, and
establish a house, even
a house of prayer,
a house of fasting,
a house of faith,
a house of learning,
a house of glory,
a house of order,
a house of God.

June 5, 2018

We Kneel Before The Altar

We kneel before
the altar
all dressed in
robes of white

We covenant with
our Father
to grow within
the light.

June 5, 2018

It's All Relative

It's all relative
at the temple
and it is for relatives
we are here

To find our ancestors
and do their work
so with them
we may be near.

March 6, 2018

Psalms 23:6

Surely goodness and mercy shall
follow me all the days of my life:
and I will dwell in the house
of the Lord for ever.

May 31, 2018

Heaven

If heaven could be
just like this
I could not,
would not
ask for more.

October 8, 1995

Isaiah 2:2-3

And it shall come to pass
in the last days, that the mountain
of the Lord's house shall be established
in the top of the mountains, and
shall be exalted above the hills;
and all nations shall flow unto it.

And many people shall go and say,
Come ye, and let us go up to the
mountain of the Lord, to the house
of the God of Jacob; and he will
teach us of his ways, and we will
walk in his paths: for out of Zion
shall go forth the law, and the word
of the Lord from Jerusalem.

June 12, 2018

Made in the USA
Columbia, SC
02 December 2020